BE NATURALLY CURIO

The Adventures of Carbon

This course was written by
Naturally Curious Expert
Valerie Grosso

*Valerie is a microbiologist who is curious about all the
microscopic things that make up our world.*

Printed by CreateSpace

ISBN 978-1-942403-04-3

www.benaturallycurious.com

Many activities in this book make use of printed materials. If you prefer not to cut them directly from this book, please visit the URL listed below and enter the code for a supplemental PDF containing all printable materials.

URL: www.benaturallycurious.com/carbon-printables/

password: **cycle**

Table of Contents

Required materials: Scissors, glue, small objects for board game (rocks, figurines), one coin, three to five packets of active dry yeast, narrow-mouthed plastic or glass bottle, balloon, measuring cup (for pouring), warm water, kitchen thermometer, sugar, salt

Carbon Cal Travels the World

Have you ever gone on a trip? Maybe on the train, maybe in a car or plane? You probably went to a new place and did new things—things you didn't do at home.

Today we are going to go on a trip with our friend Carbon Cal. Carbon Cal is an atom, a very small thing with a nucleus and electrons. As you learned in the story about Ellie the Electron, atoms can come together because of their lonely electrons and form molecules. Some of the molecules you made had an atom called CARBON.

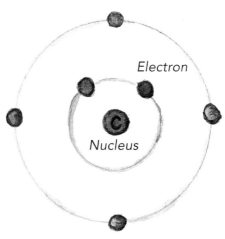

CARBON ATOM

Today we will be following along with one carbon atom, Carbon Cal, to see what different kinds of molecules he can make. As we will see, Carbon Cal, along with other carbon atoms, is a very important part of Planet Earth. We can find Carbon Cal and his carbon atom friends all over the planet! All living things, as well as many nonliving things, contain carbon! So let's grab our suitcases and go meet Carbon Cal!

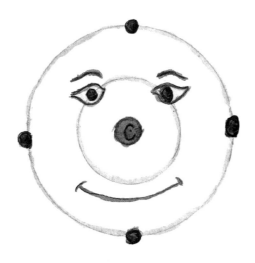

All living things, as well as many nonliving things, contain carbon!

We first find Carbon Cal up in the sky. What do you think is in the sky?

What do you think air is made of?

Can we see it?

Can we feel it?

Wave your hands around! If you feel it, something must be there. That something is molecules! But what kind of molecules? There are a whole bunch of different kinds, but one kind is called CARBON DIOXIDE. And that's where we will first find Carbon Cal. He's found two of his friends,

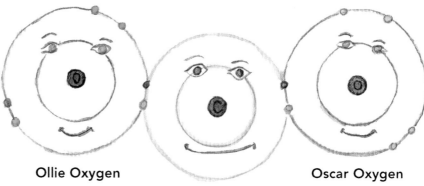

Ollie Oxygen

Carbon Cal

Oscar Oxygen

Ollie Oxygen and Oscar Oxygen. Carbon Cal had four lonely electrons, and Ollie and Oscar each had two lonely electrons. Their lonely electrons all joined up to make a molecule with Carbon Cal and Ollie and Oscar.

What do you think a molecule of carbon dioxide does up in the air? Does it stay still? NO! It moves around. It floats here, it floats there, and sometimes, if there is a strong wind, it goes really, really fast. Can you move around like our carbon dioxide molecule?

After a while, Carbon Cal's carbon dioxide molecule gets close to the ground. It gets so close to the ground, in fact, that it bumps into a leaf of a plant. Then something special happens! Plant leaves LOVE carbon dioxide molecules. When one bumps into a leaf, the plant can suck the carbon dioxide into the leaf! Whooosh! Into the leaf goes Carbon Cal with his carbon dioxide molecule!

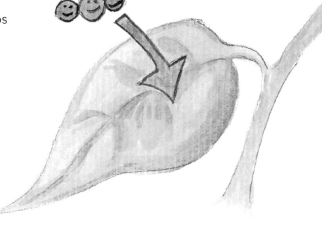

Inside the leaf, Carbon Cal meets all kinds of interesting molecules. Some are molecules called *enzymes* that do work for the plant. One type of work they do is make food for the plant! Unlike you and me, plants don't eat vegetables or bread—they make their own food! Can you guess what they use to make the food? Carbon dioxide molecules! These special worker enzymes take energy from sunlight and use it to combine the atoms in the carbon dioxide molecule with some other atoms to make a new molecule we all love— a SUGAR molecule!

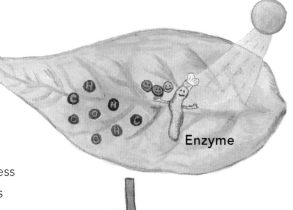

Enzyme

As you can see, this sugar molecule has Carbon Cal and the two oxygen atoms, and it also has extra carbon atoms and extra oxygen atoms and even some hydrogen atoms. The process of turning carbon dioxide and energy from sunlight into sugar is called PHOTOSYNTHESIS.

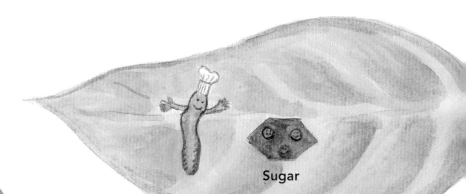

Sugar

Plants use photosynthesis to turn carbon dioxide and energy from the sun into sugar molecules.

Carbon Cal is very happy to be part of the new sugar molecule, and he stays in the plant until suddenly a very hungry moose walks by and MUNCH!...gobbles up Cal's plant! Now, Carbon Cal's sugar molecule is in the body of the moose! This moose needs to walk a long distance and uses sugar molecules for energy. The moose PULLS energy out of the sugar molecule, which makes all the atoms switch around again. Carbon Cal is now back to being part of a carbon dioxide molecule! Animals like us and like moose are NOT like plants—we want to get rid of our carbon dioxide molecules. When we breathe out, carbon dioxide molecules go back out into the air! When living things take energy from molecules like sugar and breathe out carbon dioxide, it is called RESPIRATION. Can you follow where Carbon Call goes in the pictures below?

Living things use sugar molecules for energy and breathe out carbon dioxide in a process called *respiration*.

Carbon Cal is floating around again—up, down, and around mountains until…uh oh… there he goes, getting close to the ground again. What do you think will happen? You got it! A plant! Whoosh! In he goes again, and part of a sugar molecule he becomes. This time, however, the plant is not eaten by a moose. Instead, when winter comes, the plant dies and all of the plant's molecules, like Carbon Cal's sugar molecule, go into the soil. Sugar molecules are great food for almost all living things. Who do you think might find Carbon Cal's sugar molecule in the soil? Well, maybe an insect, or maybe MICROBES, such as bacteria and fungi. Both insects and microbes like to use sugars for food, and after they get energy from it, guess what they let go of? You got it! Carbon dioxide!

What are you CURIOUS about?

Back Carbon Cal goes into the sky...round and round. I bet you can guess what happens eventually...yep, back into a plant and then pulled into a sugar molecule. This time, Carbon Cal's carbon dioxide molecule is taken up and turned into sugar by an oak tree. After a while, people come and cut down the oak tree to use some of it as firewood. Fire is another way of getting energy from molecules. That's what happens here. Fire releases energy, and the sugar is turned back to carbon dioxide, and BACK INTO THE AIR goes Carbon Cal!

Burning wood, oil, or gas for energy also releases carbon dioxide.

 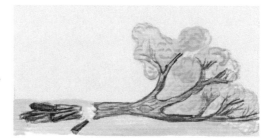

This happens whenever we burn things, whether they be wood, gas, or oil. In fact, parts of plants and animals can mix with the soil to form **SEDIMENTS**. After a very long time, these sediments get changed into things like gas and oil, which people burn for heat and energy.

Is there anywhere else on this planet for Carbon Cal to explore? Let's think—Cal's been to plants, animals, and microbes on the land...What about the ocean? If you were Cal, wouldn't you want to explore the ocean?

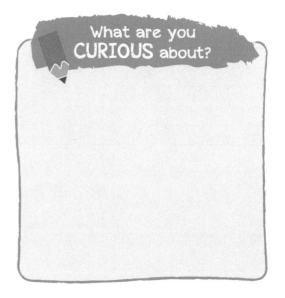

What are you CURIOUS about?

That's just what Cal does next. As he zooms down to the surface of the ocean, he bumps into phytoplankton (small green living things) that do just what plants do—they suck in CO_2 and use the sun's energy to make sugar molecules. But this time, when the phytoplankton use the sugar energy, Cal doesn't go straight back to CO_2. Instead, he becomes part of a similar molecule called BICARBONATE. Carbon Cal takes a free ride around the ocean waves as part of the bicarbonate molecule until he eventually gets snatched up by a crab. This crab uses the bicarbonate molecule to help make its protective shell. To make the shell hard, an atom of calcium must be added to the bicarbonate, producing CALCIUM CARBONATE. Cal spends a long time as part of the crab's shell until, eventually, the crab's shell gets left at the bottom of the ocean. Very slowly, the calcium carbonate molecules make their way back into the ocean water and become bicarbonate again. After a VERY long time, Cal's bicarbonate molecule comes back to the surface of the ocean and SWOOP! Back up into the air he goes as a carbon dioxide molecule!

Oh, the adventures Carbon Cal has had! First the air, then part of a plant, an animal, and a microbe, and then finally as part of the ocean! Who knows where he is off to next or where he is hiding now? Next time you go outside, look at all the things around you and try to figure out where Carbon Cal might have been—and might be now!

In the ocean, carbon dioxide turns into a bicarbonate molecule.

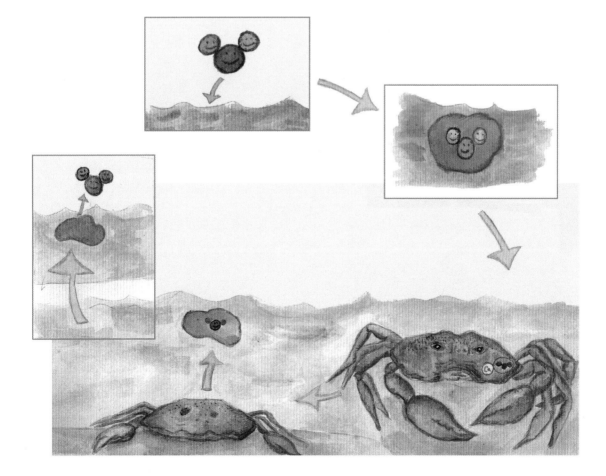

ACTIVITY
1

Where Does Carbon Cal Belong?

INSTRUCTIONS

Cut out each of Carbon Cal's molecule disguises on page 27. Where do you think each one belongs?

Glue each form of Carbon Cal onto the picture on page 29. Is there more than one place for some of the molecules? You can show a molecule LEAVING or ENTERING a place by drawing an arrow into or out of a picture. For example, you might glue a CO_2 next to an animal's mouth, with an arrow showing that the CO_2 is coming OUT!

MATERIALS
- scissors
- glue

PARENT GUIDE

MOLECULE	WHERE FOUND
CO_2 (Carbon Dioxide)	Air, coming out of living things, going into plants, going into and out of the ocean, coming out of fires
Bicarbonate	Ocean
Calcium Carbonate	Shells
Sugar	Living things (plants, animals, microbes, fungi), firewood

ACTIVITY
2

Can You Be Carbon Cal?

INSTRUCTIONS

Now we know lots of places where Carbon Cal can be found. Let's imagine we ARE the molecules that Carbon Cal is part of. Read the list of molecules below. When you read each molecule, act out where that molecule is found. For example, if CO_2 is read, you could act out the wind swooping around. If a sugar molecule is read, you can act out any living thing—animal, plant, or microbe. Have a parent or friend guess what you are acting out!

For more of a challenge, after each thing you act out, figure out what Carbon Cal might do next (where he might go) and act THAT out. For example, if you were just acting out CO_2, you could then act out a sugar molecule in a plant.

PARENT GUIDE

Molecules to Act Out	Locations to Act Out
CO_2	Air, being taken up by a plant, being breathed out by an animal or other living thing, going into or out of the ocean
Sugar	Plant, animal, microbe
Bicarbonate	Ocean water
Calcium carbonate	Shell

Bonus: Make Your Own Carbon Adventure!

Without using words, act out a trip for Carbon Cal. Let your parents guess each stop on the trip! Have them write down each "stop." Then see if they get them all right. Make sure the stops are in the same order that Carbon Cal would travel!

Parents and friends can use the Travel Journal on page 14 to guess which stops you are acting out.

Travel Journal

Carbon Cal's Travel Itinerary #1:

1. _____

2. _____

3. _____

4. _____

5. _____

Carbon Cal's Travel Itinerary #2:

1. _____

2. _____

3. _____

4. _____

5. _____

ACTIVITY
3

The Hunt for Carbon Cal

INSTRUCTIONS

Take a walk in your neighborhood and find some places where Carbon Cal might be hiding! Print out the Field Notebook on page 16. Make sure to take careful notes—describe where he might be and what type of molecule he might be part of. Make sure to draw what you see! Explain why you think each thing might contain Carbon Cal.

PARENT GUIDE

POSSIBLE OBJECTS	CARBON-CONTAINING MOLECULE
Animal	Contains sugar, releases CO_2
Plant	Contains sugar, releases CO_2, takes in CO_2
Other living things (mushrooms, lichens, etc.)	Contain sugar, release CO_2
Plant matter in soil	Contains sugar
Microbes in soil	Contain sugar, release CO_2
Water	Any plants or animals in the water contain sugar, bicarbonate if ocean water
Shells	Calcium carbonate
Rocks	Many (but not all) rocks have carbon in them
Wood	Part of a plant, sugar

ACTIVITY
3

Field Notebook

Object	Sketch	How is Carbon Cal hiding here (what type of molecule)?	Explain why you think Carbon Cal might be here.

It's a Carbon Cycle Race!

INSTRUCTIONS

It's time to race around the planet and its atmosphere with Carbon Cal! Your mission is to visit each one of Carbon Cal's favorite spots as fast as you can. First, you will need to cut out cards for all of Carbon Cal's favorite spots. For each player, cut out one of each type of card (9 different types in total). If you have more than three players, you can make more cards by printing out an extra copy of pages 31 and 33.

MATERIALS

- one small object for each player (figurine, rock, etc.)
- a coin
- scissors

Now that you have the cards ready, it's time to race! Using the gameboard on page 35, players start by placing their tokens on CO_2 (in the sky). Don't pick up any cards yet. Starting with the youngest player, follow one of the arrows (each player can choose which one) from CO_2 to one of Carbon Cal's next stops. When you get there, pick up the corresponding card for that stop. Now it's the next player's turn. Players continue to follow arrows, moving one spot during each turn. If there is a choice of arrows with the letters "H" (heads) and "T" (tails), flip a coin and follow the arrow with the corresponding letter. Sometimes you may need to flip a coin twice in the same turn to get to the next stop. Keep following arrows from stop to stop (one stop at each turn) until you have collected cards from all the stops. The first player to collect all the cards wins!

ACTIVITY 5

Make CO$_2$ in Your Kitchen!

We've learned that living things such as moose, plants, and microbes can have Carbon Cal in the form of sugar molecules. We also learned that when these living things take energy out of the sugar, the molecule is changed and CO$_2$ is made. This is what we (and and other living things) breathe out!

Sugar molecules

Today we will watch some living things breathe out CO$_2$. We will use baking yeast—the stuff used to make bread. Yeast are very small (microscopic) fungi that are related to big fungi like mushrooms. When we buy yeast in a store, they are in an inactive form (sort of like sleeping). We need to wake them up and make them active. Today we will do that by adding warm water to the yeast.

When living things become active, they need sugar molecules for energy! So we will mix our yeast with sugar.

How can we tell if our yeast take energy from the sugar?

Well, what did we say the yeast do to the sugar molecules? What is breathed out of the yeast? Yep, you've got it—CO$_2$! We can see if the yeast are taking energy from the sugar by seeing if they turn it into CO$_2$!

But how will we see the CO$_2$ if it's invisible? For this, we'll use a little trick. CO$_2$ is a gas, and sugar is a solid. We'll mix our sugar and yeast and then quickly cover our bottle with a balloon. Then we'll wait to see whether MORE gas is made. If more gas is made, our balloon will inflate!

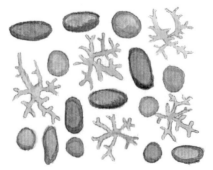

Microbes

ACTIVITY
5

Make CO$_2$ in Your Kitchen!

INSTRUCTIONS

Scientists like to come up with hypotheses—possible explanations—for things they are curious about. We will test some hypotheses today with our experiments.

EXPERIMENT 1

Hypothesis: Active (warm) yeast make CO$_2$ from sugar.

1. Stretch your balloon a few times in all directions to make sure it's nice and flexible. Then put it aside.

2. Pour one packet of active dry yeast into your bottle.

3. In a measuring cup (or something that is easy to pour from), heat one cup of water in the microwave (or on a stove) until it is roughly 110 degrees F.

4. Pour the warm water into the bottle.

5. Add 3 tablespoons of sugar to the bottle.

6. Stretch the balloon over the mouth of the bottle.

7. Watch the balloon to see if it inflates. This may take a little while, so you may want to check back every 15 minutes or so.

8. Fill in your Experimental Journal on page 21. Be sure to fill in each column. Record your observations in the last column.

Scientists like to explore other hypotheses using the same equipment. Make sure to rinse out your bottle between each experiment! Let's look at some other hypotheses we can test.

> ## MATERIALS
> - active dry yeast
> - empty narrow-mouthed plastic or glass bottle
> - balloon
> - measuring cup
> - warm water
> - thermometer
> - sugar
> - salt

ACTIVITY
5

Make CO$_2$ in Your Kitchen!

INSTRUCTIONS (continued)

EXPERIMENT 2

Hypothesis: Active (warm) yeast will not make CO$_2$ if we give them salt instead of sugar.

Perform Experiment 2 EXACTLY LIKE Experiment 1, EXCEPT add salt instead of sugar. Take notes in the second row of your Experimental Journal and observe your results!

EXPERIMENT 3

Hypothesis: We need active (warm) yeast to turn sugar into CO$_2$. Cold yeast won't yield the same results.

To test this hypothesis, perform the experiment just like Experiment 1, EXCEPT use cold water (from the tap or your fridge) instead of warm water. Make sure to measure the temperature of the water and fill in the third row of your Experimental Journal.

You can use the same equipment to test other hypotheses, too. What hypothesis would you like to test? Here are some ideas:

- What would happen if you add less sugar? State your hypothesis and design your experiment!

- What would happen if you use really hot water instead of warm water? State your hypothesis and design your experiment!

In each case, fill out a row in your Experimental Journal, taking notes about everything you mixed together and your observations. If you didn't get the result you expected, you get to be even more of a scientist—come up with a new hypothesis!

After you have completed a whole series of experiments, look at your results. Which conditions produced the most CO$_2$? Which conditions produced the least CO$_2$? Why do you think this is the case?

Experimental Journal

				Experiment Number
				Hypothesis
				Yeast Added?
				Water Temp.
				Sugar Added?
				Other Substance Added?
				Observations

Curiosity Connector

Here are some links to help you follow your curiosity!

- Another description of Earth's carbon cycle:
  http://www.kidsgeo.com/geography-for-kids/0159-the-carbon-cycle.php

- Games and videos to learn about the carbon cycle:
  http://www.neok12.com/Carbon-Cycle.htm

- Cool activities and instruction on the carbon cycle and climate change:
  http://climatekids.nasa.gov/menu/carbons-travels/

- Fun games and videos about the carbon cycle with an emphasis on climate change:
  http://www.amnh.org/explore/ology/climatechange

- Climate change instruction for kids:
  http://www.epa.gov/climatechange/kids/basics/today/carbon-dioxide.html

What are you CURIOUS about?

Glossary

BICARBONATE – A molecule that contains carbon and is found in ocean water

CALCIUM CARBONATE – A molecule that contains carbon and is what shells are made of

CARBON DIOXIDE (CO_2) – A molecule made from one carbon and two oxygen atoms. Living things breathe out CO_2, and plants also use it to make food.

FOSSIL FUELS – Part of the ground, such as soil and coal, that is made up of decaying plants and other living things. Fossil fuels contain lots of carbon and lots of energy!

MICROBES – Microscopic living things such as bacteria and fungi

PHOTOSYNTHESIS – The process used by plants and some microbes to turn carbon dioxide and the sun's energy into sugar molecules

RESPIRATION – The process used by living things to take energy from sugar molecules and breathe out carbon dioxide molecules

SEDIMENTS – Small pieces of rocks and minerals that are moved around by water and wind

SUGAR – A molecule that contains carbon and is found in all living things. Living things use sugar molecules for energy!

Tools for Your Tool Kit

Let's make the ideas you learned today part of your life tool kit. Remember to print out some blank tool kit pages and tape or glue on today's tools.

1. When living things breathe out AND when we burn things, what type of molecule is released into the air?

   _____

   Add CARBON DIOXIDE (CO_2) to your tool kit.

2. When plants take up Carbon Cal in the form of CO_2, they combine it with energy from sunlight to make sugar. What is the name of this process?

   _____

   Add PHOTOSYNTHESIS to your tool kit.

3. When living things take energy from sugar molecules and breathe CO_2 back out, this process is called _____ .

   Add RESPIRATION to your tool kit.

4. When CO_2 hits ocean water, it is changed into which type of molecule?

   _____

   Add BICARBONATE to your tool kit.

5. The shells of sea creatures like to keep Carbon Cal in the form of which molecule?

   _____

   Add CALCIUM CARBONATE to your tool kit.

Tools for Your Tool Kit (continued)

CO2 (Carbon Dioxide)

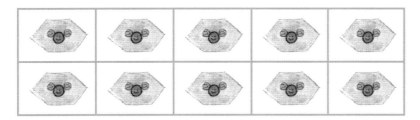

Sugar

Bicarbonate

Calcium Carbonate

Printout for Activity 1: Where Does Carbon Cal Belong?

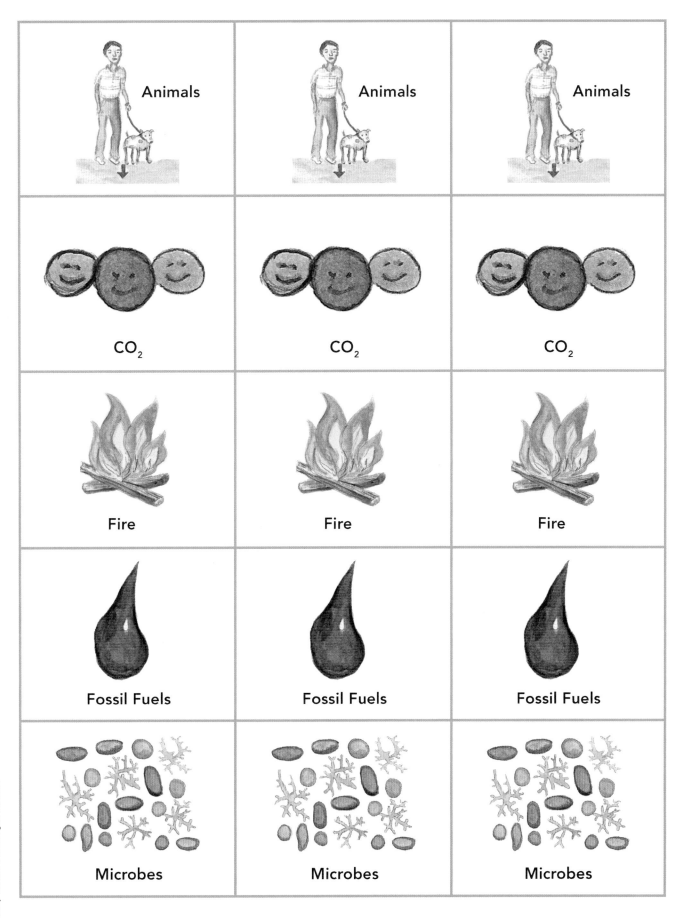

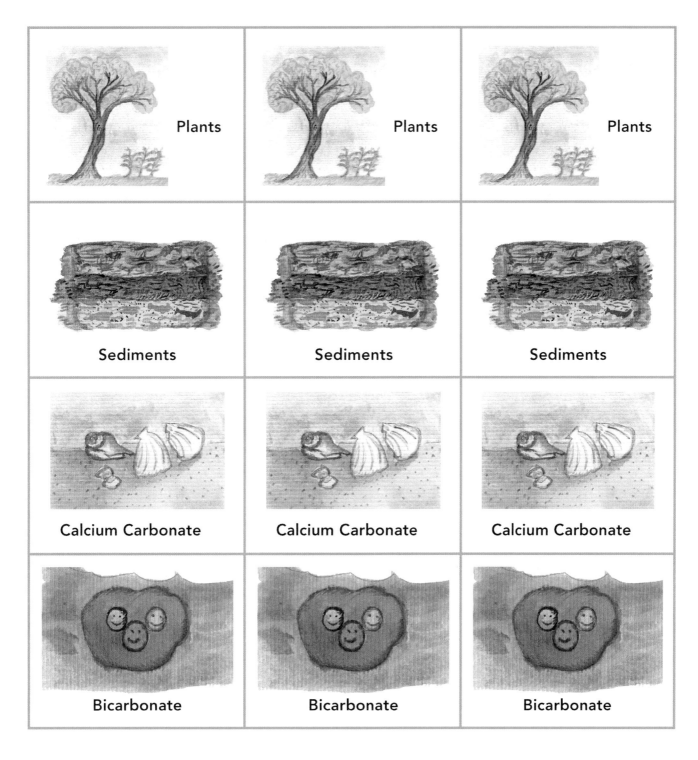

Gameboard for Activity 4: It's a Carbon Cycle Race!

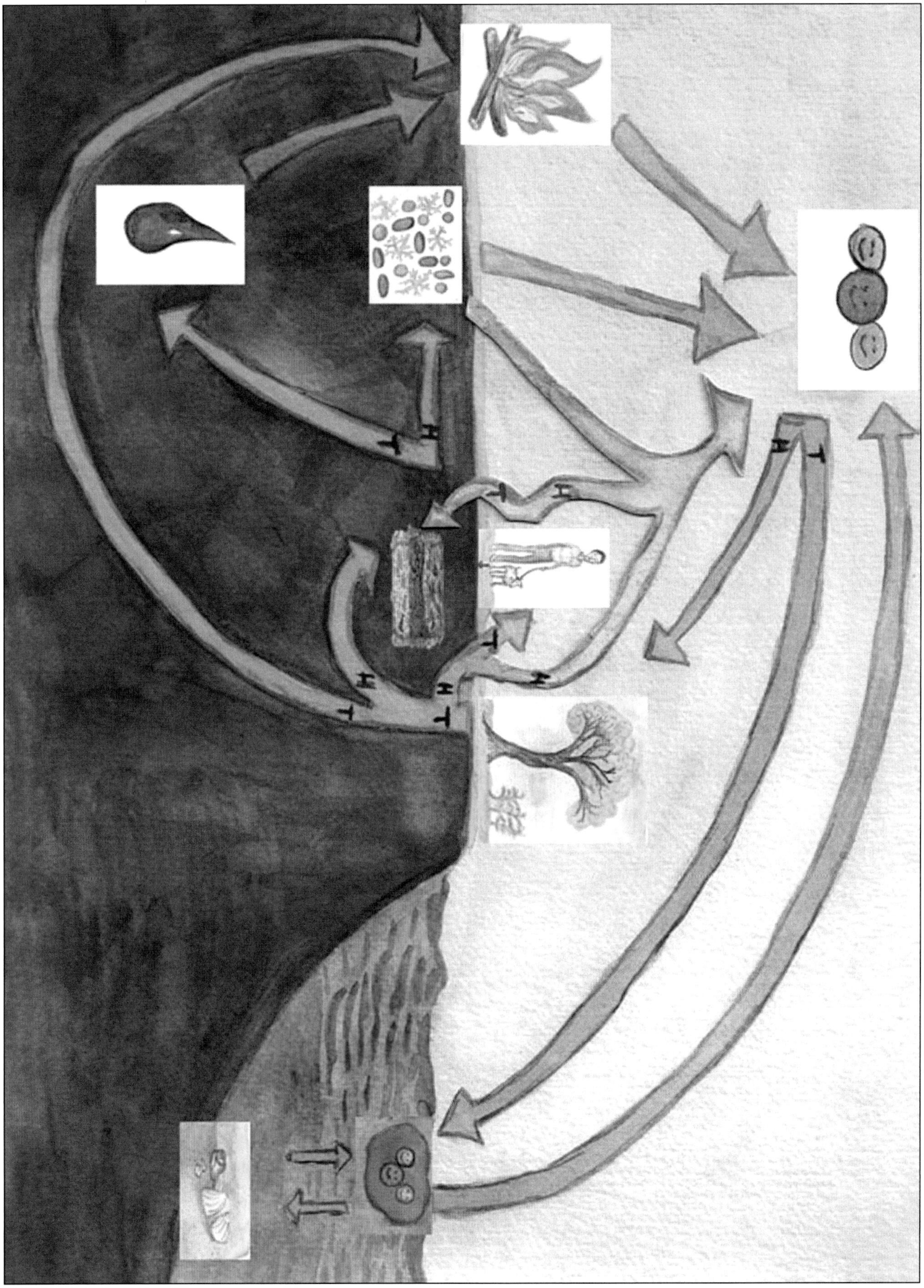

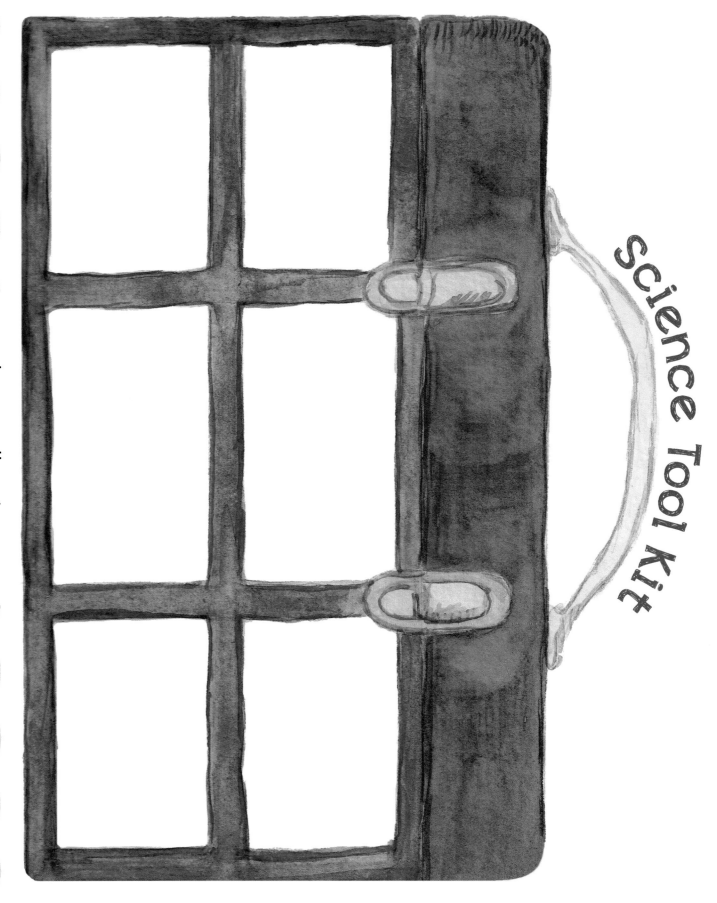

Science Tool Kit